IMAGES
of America

LONG ISLAND
AIRPORTS

FORT H. G. WRIGHT, FISHERS ISLAND, C. 1925. Although not physically on Long Island, Fishers Island is part of Suffolk County. It started off as a small military airfield with spotter planes for the coastal defense forts on Long Island's east end. It has now evolved into a general aviation airport with two paved 2,000-foot runways. Now called Elizabeth Field, it sees moderate usage during the summer months.

IMAGES
of America

LONG ISLAND
AIRPORTS

Joshua Stoff

ARCADIA

First published 2004

Published by Arcadia Publishing,
Charleston SC, Chicago IL, Portsmouth NH, San Francisco CA

Printed in Great Britain

Library of Congress Catalog Card Number: 2004108656

For all general information, contact Arcadia Publishing:
Telephone 843-853-2070
Fax 843-853-0044
E-mail sales@arcadiapublishing.com
For customer service and orders:
Toll-free 1-888-313-2665

Visit us on the Internet at www.arcadiapublishing.com

*To Jill—I am one of the few lucky ones
who got to marry his best friend.*

THE AUTHOR, CORAM AIRPARK, C. 1985. This small dirt strip closed in 1985. As with most Long Island airfields, the site is now a housing development.

CONTENTS

PREFACE

This work concerns itself with airports on geographical Long Island—that is, Brooklyn, Queens, Nassau, and Suffolk Counties. The airports are listed alphabetically within each chapter, by their last or most recent name. Any photographs not otherwise credited are from the collection of the Cradle of Aviation Museum. This work briefly covers the history and has photographs of 70 of the 82 airports known to have existed on Long Island since 1909. Sadly, the rest are lost to history.

A book of such scope as this could not have been written without the support of many people. When I embarked on this project, I expected that nearly all of the information and photographs could be found in the library and archives of the Cradle of Aviation Museum. Such was not the case; many airfields proved elusive, and pinning down any firm information or finding photographs was difficult. Thus, I called on the support of many individuals and organizations. I could not have completed this project without the following: Lee Roche, Wally Broge, Florence Ogg, Robin Strong, Chuck Webber, Mike Myers, Bob Schmidt, Gene Oshrin, Van Field, Bart Spadaro, Parker Wickham, Barbara Forde, Lou Mancuso, Peter Truesdale, Michael Brosnan, Lynn MacDonald, Walt Winnicki, Leo Polaski, the Port Authority of New York and New Jersey, and the Northrop Grumman History Center.

INTRODUCTION

In centuries past, no seaport city could hope to thrive unless it had a well-developed harbor and docking facilities in order to bring ships from across the seas safely into port. In the 19th century, as railroads spread their steel web across the United States, towns and cities sprang up around rail centers and marshalling yards. Towns lucky enough to have a station on the line grew, often at amazing rates.

Once the air age arrived in the 20th century, all the major cities of the world developed flying fields and, later, airports to serve the evolving passenger and cargo craft of the sky. Such aircraft soon crossed continents and oceans at startling speeds, compared to those attainable but a few decades earlier. Thus the airport became a vital part of the transportation system, one central to the life of every city, connecting it to the world at large.

The story of the airports on Long Island began in much the same way as elsewhere, with small open "flying fields" and crudely built hangars. It was from such scruffy, mud-covered fields that the first airmail services began. These open-cockpit biplanes, with no radios, often flew in appalling weather conditions. Gradually this service spread across the country, and more airfields were needed, some now with lighting for night operations. By the late 1920s, a system of lighted airways with radio beacons guiding the way spanned the continent, and with it came passenger service. By the end of World War I, just 15 years after the Wrights first flew, there were about 600 official "landing fields" in America. However, a close look at this list reveals many to be golf or country clubs, others to be for "water machines" only, and just 13 municipal flying fields in the entire country. By 1927, the number of civil airports jumped to 1,036, and by the mid-1930s, the height of the post-Lindbergh flying fever, the number had doubled. Thus from these simple beginnings—a small number of biplanes flying out of rudimentary fields—the American air transport system has grown to its present stage.

The birth and stunning growth of the American airport system can be seen and understood by looking at what happened in just one place—Long Island, New York. In fewer than 100 years, aviation arrived, boomed, and evolved on Long Island. During that time, Long Island helped transform aviation from a dangerous sport to a viable means of transportation. It has also produced a large portion of the nation's aerial arsenal in times of war. The many record-setting and historic flights that transpired on Long Island, and the many aviation companies that developed there, helped make aviation the integral part of our world that it is today. Long Island was geographically a natural airfield; the island itself is ideally placed at the eastern edge of the United States, at the western edge of the Atlantic Ocean, and adjacent to America's most populous city. This made it the ideal focal point for most transatlantic and transcontinental flights. Furthermore, the central area of Long Island's Nassau County, known as the Hempstead Plains, was the only natural prairie east of the Allegheny Mountains. This proved to be an ideal flying field, treeless and flat, with only tall grasses and scattered farmhouses. Combined with good rail access and roadways, and located within easy reach of New York City financial backing, the Hempstead Plains were to become the scene of intense aviation activity for 50 years.

By 1909, the first daring flights were made from these Hempstead Plains. Because the flat, open landscape made a natural airfield, famous aviator Glenn Curtiss brought his biplane, the Golden Flyer, there. By 1910, there were three airfields operating on the Plains, and local residents began building their own airplanes. Several flying schools and aircraft factories sprang up, and Long Island soon became the center of the aviation world. This was further evidenced in 1910 and 1911, when pioneer aviators came from all over America and Europe to Long Island's grassy fields to fly at the earliest international air meets in America. By World War I, these simple flying fields had evolved into Hazelhurst and Mitchel Fields, major American centers for training army aviators and experimenting with new types of military aircraft and aviation equipment.

The period between 1918 and 1939 is known as the golden age of aviation, a time when flying went from being a dangerous sport to becoming a major commercial industry. During this colorful age, speed, distance, and other record-setting flying events became popular. As Long Island was the center of world aviation, the known limits of flight were expanded regularly in the skies over its airfields. By far the most famous aviation event to have occurred on Long Island—and in the world—during this exciting time was Charles Lindbergh's historic flight from Roosevelt Field, Long Island, to Paris in 1927. This single event revolutionized aviation as nothing else did, before or since. Lindbergh's flight was followed by many more successful transatlantic flights, to and from Long Island. By the early 1930s, Roosevelt Field was the largest and busiest civilian airfield in America, with over 150 aviation businesses and manufacturers, and over 450 planes based there. By the late 1930s, the first commercial transatlantic flights departed Long Island, albeit from the bay adjoining the new municipal airport in Queens. During this same time, Mitchel Field on Long Island became the U.S. Army's premier airfield, boasting the finest facilities and housing the newest types of fighter, bomber, and observation aircraft.

During World War II, Long Island–built aircraft clearly helped America win victory, as Allied fighter operations were dominated by locally built aircraft. Two large companies, Grumman and Republic, dominated the local defense industry, and their airfields were inevitably packed with new aircraft, just off the line and destined for combat. After the war, commercial aviation boomed on Long Island, as it did elsewhere in America, in part due to the airport act of 1946, which granted federal funds for new airport construction. It was during this time that Long Island's LaGuardia Airport steadily expanded and New York International (Kennedy) Airport was born and grew with explosive speed.

Thus, Long Island, New York, serves as an excellent microcosm of the entire history of aviation. In fact, nowhere else in America was there so much intense aviation activity confined to such a relatively small geographical area. From the first frail pioneers to today's jumbo jets, all have flown from Long Island airfields, whether they be of grass or concrete. Similarly, the evolution of the American airport can also be documented in photographs of what happened in just this one place. Over the course of aviation's first 100 years, there have been 82 airfields on Long Island. Thus, this work documents what once was. It is, in fact, the first time anyone has attempted to put so grand a story together. At one time, Long Island had the most airports of any one place in America, but sadly, most have vanished without a trace. Now, just a handful remain. However, the Long Island airports that do remain handle types of aircraft and volumes of traffic inconceivable to aviation's pioneers. Perhaps in the next 100 years, aerospace planes will depart from these same fields for suborbital flights around the world, or for voyages to ports on the Moon or Mars. Who knows what wonders the future will hold?

One
PIONEER AIRFIELDS

BELMONT PARK, ELMONT, 1910–1920. In October 1910, America's first international air meet was held on an improvised airfield at Belmont Park, a new horse-racing track. The field was chosen due to its open infield, large grandstand, visitor amenities, and good rail and road access. Here Earle Ovington lands his Bleriot monoplane.

WRIGHT BABY GRAND RACER FLYING PAST THE GRANDSTAND, BELMONT PARK, 1910. For this meet, the greatest aviators came from all over America and Europe, and they set several new records for altitude, endurance, and speed.

SANTOS DUMONT DEMOISELLE STARTING UP IN FRONT OF HANGAR ROW, BELMONT PARK, 1910. Many fine wooden hangars and several large tents were constructed just for this meet.

LOADING MAIL INTO A CURTISS JN-4, BELMONT PARK, MAY 1918. This site was again selected as a temporary airfield in 1918 for the terminus of the Washington to New York airmail route. The 200-mile flight took about four hours if the weather was good. The field remained the New York Airmail Station until 1920, when it was moved to Hazelhurst Field.

GLENWOOD COUNTRY CLUB, GLEN HEAD, 1912. In 1912, the Wright Company sent up one of its Model B planes, fitted with floats, and its pilot, Charles Wald, to set up a seaplane flying school on the north shore of Long Island. A hangar and workshop were built on the grounds of the Glenwood Country Club, with a ramp leading to Hempstead Harbor. Failure to attract any students led to the base's closure after only a few months, although many successful flights were made. (Photograph courtesy of Peter Truesdale.)

HEMPSTEAD PLAINS AIRFIELD, GARDEN CITY, 1911–1917. By 1911, the older Mineola and Nassau Boulevard fields were found to be too small, so most flying moved to this new airfield. The open expanse of the Long Island prairie known as the Hempstead Plains is evident in this photograph. It was a huge natural airfield and attracted a great number of aviators. Here a Curtiss-type biplane lifts off.

UNSUCCESSFUL ZOILO GARCIA POLYPLANE, HEMPSTEAD PLAINS FIELD, 1912. Founded by Alfred Moisant, this 650-acre field was much larger and more open than the other local airfields. In fact, it was probably the largest airfield in America at the time.

MOISANT MONOPLANE LANDING AT HEMPSTEAD PLAINS FIELD, 1913. By the summer of 1911, this field had 25 wooden hangars, 5 concrete ones, grandstands, and pylons. It was considered the finest flying field in America. Several flying schools and aircraft manufacturers came to call this field home. In 1912, the Aero Club of America moved here, and the field became an important center of experimentation.

BLERIOT-TYPE MONOPLANE, BUILT BY THE AMERICAN AEROPLANE SUPPLY HOUSE, HEMPSTEAD PLAINS, 1912. This was the largest aircraft manufacturer on Long Island at the time. In 1916, the U.S. Army took over the field, and in 1917, it was renamed Hazelhurst Field. By 1920, this same field was called Curtiss Field, and in 1929, it finally became Roosevelt Field.

MINEOLA FIELD, MINEOLA, 1909–1912. This huge, flat, open expanse of Long Island's Hempstead Plains made a natural flying field, which is why Glenn Curtiss selected the area to test his newest airplane, the Golden Flyer. Here the Golden Flyer circles over Mineola Field while winning the Scientific America Trophy for the first American flight of 25 kilometers in July 1909.

CURTISS AIRCRAFT IN FRONT OF MCLAUGHLIN'S HOTEL, MINEOLA, 1910. This local beer hall, on the north end of the field, quickly became a popular hangout for pioneer aviators. The first tents for hangars were set up in the summer of 1909, next to the Mineola Fairgrounds on Washington Avenue, which led to this also being called the Washington Avenue Field.

MINEOLA HANGAR OF THE AERONAUTICAL SOCIETY OF NEW YORK, 1910. In 1910, the Aeronautical Society of New York built a 150-foot-long hangar (huge for its day), and Mineola Field soon became one of the most important American centers for aeronautical experimentation.

DR. HENRY WALDEN IN HIS MODEL 9, MINEOLA, 1910. Walden built and flew the first American monoplane at Mineola in 1909. Several new, important types of aircraft were built here, and many new records were set here as well. The field measured one-half of a mile wide by three-fourths of a mile long, with a total of six wooden hangars.

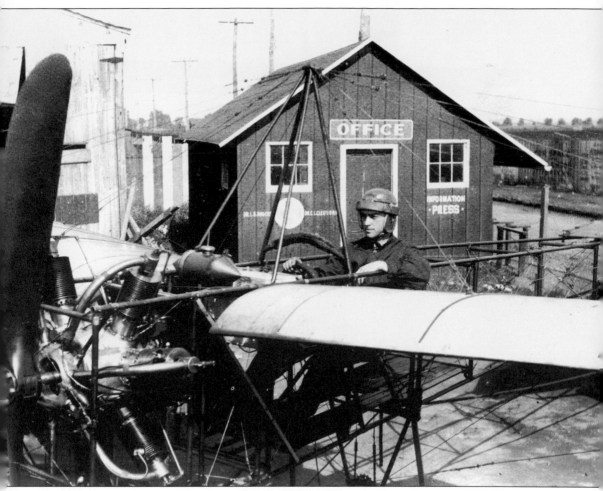

ALL-METAL MONOPLANE, BUILT BY WALTER FAIRCHILD, AT THE ENTRANCE TO MINEOLA FIELD, 1912. By the end of 1912, Mineola Field was found to be too small, so all flying moved a mile east to the huge new Hempstead Plains Field. The site of Mineola Field has since been developed into a county courthouse complex. (Photograph courtesy of John Underwood.)

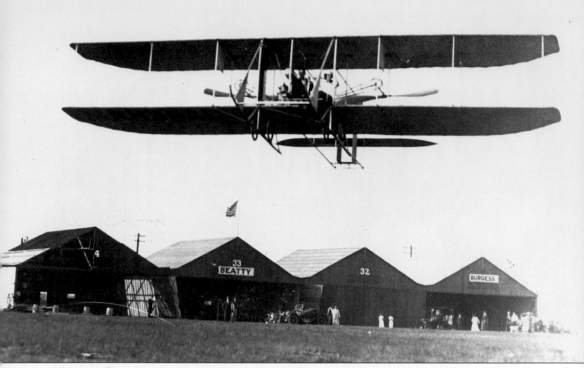

NASSAU BOULEVARD AIRFIELD, GARDEN CITY, 1910–1913. Due to the small confines of Mineola Field, a new field was constructed in nearby Garden City. At the time, this 350-acre field was one of the finest flying fields in America, featuring 31 wooden hangars, 5 grandstands, workshops, a refreshment stand, and a headquarters building. Here a Wright B takes off in front of hangar row.

QUEEN MARTIN BIPLANE AT THE NASSAU BOULEVARD AIR MEET, 1911. In October 1911, this field hosted a major international air meet. This meet was notable for being the first in which women competed with men. It was also where the U.S. Army made its first public flying appearance.

A WRIGHT B ON THE NASSAU BOULEVARD FLIGHT LINE, 1911. By 1913, the field was also seen as too small, and the land too valuable, so all flying activity moved over to the new, much larger Hempstead Plains Field.

Earle Ovington Landing His Bleriot, Nassau Boulevard, 1911. Ovington made the first U.S. airmail flights, though just to neighboring Mineola, at the 1911 meet. The Nassau Boulevard field stretched between the Nassau Boulevard and Merillon Avenue railroad stations. It was sold for use as a housing development in 1913.

SHEEPSHEAD BAY RACETRACK, BROOKLYN, 1910–1916. Located on the infield of a horse-racing track in Brooklyn, this airfield was used on a fairly regular basis for air meets and demonstration flights, due to its large grandstand, open space, and visitor amenities. Here a Wright B prepares for flight in 1910.

CAL RODGERS TAKING OFF IN THE WRIGHT EX "VIN FIZ" FROM SHEEPSHEAD BAY AT THE START OF THE FIRST TRANSCONTINENTAL FLIGHT. Departing on September 17, 1911, Rodgers arrived in California 49 days and 11 crashes later. At this temporary airfield, no structures were built for housing airplanes, so tents were used.

LINCOLN BEACHY RACING BARNEY OLDFIELD, SHEEPSHEAD BAY, 1914. As this was the closest airfield to Manhattan in the early years of flight, it was an ideal site for aeronautic demonstrations.

Two

SEAPLANE BASES

AMITYVILLE SEAPLANE BASE, AMITYVILLE, 1927–1932. This base on the Great South Bay was run by the Fairchild Company of Farmingdale. It was used to mount their new planes on floats, and to test new types of flying boats. In this aerial view, five new Fairchilds can be seen anchored in the channel, in front of the seaplane hangar under construction.

CANADIAN EXPORT FAIRCHILD FC-2W, FITTED WITH FLOATS ON THE MARINE RAILWAY, 1929. The Amityville Seaplane Base operated out of the Hulse Brothers boatyard.

BABYLON SEAPLANE BASE, BABYLON, 1935–1947. This small base on the Great South Bay featured five floatplanes and one hangar. The McKinley pneumatic floats produced here were an unsuccessful attempt to adapt the balloon-tire principle to seaplane floats. The floats were made of airship fabric in place of aluminum. Here a Piper Cub sits on these floats at Babylon in 1939. The floats could also serve as skis on snow.

BAYPORT SEAPLANE BASE, BAYPORT, 1930–1935. Due to the calm conditions and wide-open expanse, Long Island's Great South Bay was a natural flying field for seaplanes. This base was located on the strand at the foot of Edgewater Avenue. The few planes based here mainly served to give rides to summer tourists or shuttle people to Fire Island. Here a Fairchild KR-34C lands on the bay near Bayport in 1934.

BROOKLYN SKYPORT, BROOKLYN, 1928–1947. Located on the western edge of Barren Island at Mill Basin, the Skyport rarely housed more than eight seaplanes. There was one metal hangar, a dock, ramp, and the open expanse of Jamaica Bay spread out before it. Here an Aeronca C-3 sits on the seaplane ramp *c.* 1935.

SIKORSKY S-37 ON FLOATS, ON THE BEACH AT BROOKLYN SKYPORT, 1929. Apparently this base was most active in the late 1920s and early 1930s as a smuggling center, using seaplanes to rendezvous with ships at sea during Prohibition. This aircraft was modified for use in South America as an airliner in the late 1920s.

COLLEGE POINT SEAPLANE BASE, QUEENS, 1925–1957. This base on Flushing Bay was developed in the mid-1920s as the flying field for the newly formed EDO float company. From the 1920s through the 1950s, EDO was the world's largest manufacturer of seaplane and amphibian floats; thus, the base was usually quite busy. Here we see the hangars and factory of EDO c. 1930.

CANADIAN BELLANCA FREIGHTER BEING SERVICED AT THE COLLEGE POINT SEAPLANE BASE, 1934. This base had excellent seaplane facilities for its day, including two hangars, ramps, docks, moorings, fuel, and a two-mile, unobstructed flying field.

ISLAND PARK SEAPLANE BASE, ISLAND PARK, 1946–1959. Located on the southwestern shore of Island Park on Reynolds Channel, this small base was operated by Thomas Pryor. It consisted of three Piper Cubs on floats, which operated off the dock in Pryor's backyard. Seaplane instruction and sightseeing rides formed the bulk of the business. The operation lasted until seaplanes were banned from Nassau County's south shore, due to a collision with a boater. Here a Cub is tied to Pryor's dock c. 1950. (Photograph courtesy of Mrs. Thomas Pryor.)

LONG BEACH SEAPLANE BASE, LONG BEACH, 1921–1959. In the 1920s, the Aeromarine Company of New Jersey operated a commuter airline service between New York City and various points in the Northeast. Long Beach was on Route 3 and was one of four stops between Manhattan and Easthampton. The line lasted until 1925 and was used both by commuters and people heading to resort destinations. This base, complete with hangar, was on Reynolds Channel, adjacent to the Long Beach Yacht Club. Some seaplane flying continued through the 1950s. Here two Aeromarine 75s are anchored off Long Beach in 1922.

PORT JEFFERSON SEAPLANE BASE, PORT JEFFERSON, 1934–1942. Basically a seaplane anchorage, this base had no structures but was still a recognized facility. Located at the southwest end of Port Jefferson Harbor, adjacent to the town, the base had at least one mile of smooth, open water running to the north. There was a marine railway and ramp available in the neighboring boatyard so aircraft could be hauled on land for repairs. Here a Waco J-5 prepares to take off in Port Jefferson Harbor *c.* 1935.

PORT WASHINGTON SEAPLANE BASE, PORT WASHINGTON, 1916–1993. Due to its frontage along a large protected body of water and its proximity to New York City, Port Washington, on Manhasset Bay, was a mecca for seaplanes through the 1930s. Here a Curtiss MF flying boat rests in front of its Port Washington hangar in 1918.

VIEW OF MANHASSET BAY AND PORT WASHINGTON, LOOKING NORTHWEST, C. 1920. In the lower right are private seaplane hangars where local "Gold Coast" millionaires kept their Curtiss, Loening, and Grumman amphibians for commuter use.

CURTISS R3C RACING SEAPLANE, PORT WASHINGTON, 1926. Between 1916 and 1931, the Curtiss Aircraft Corporation kept a hangar here, where all new models of their seaplanes were tested.

AMERICAN AERONAUTICAL S-56 AMPHIBIAN ON THE RAMP IN FRONT OF THEIR FACTORY, PORT WASHINGTON, 1929. In 1929, the American Aeronautical Corporation, a division of Savoia Marchetti, built a major seaplane base on a 16-acre parcel on the Manhasset Isle peninsula. It had a large concrete-and-steel hangar, factory space, and a seaplane ramp. Several types of amphibians and seaplanes were built here through 1931.

PAN AMERICAN SIKORSKY S-42 TAXIING INTO PORT WASHINGTON, 1938. After American Aeronautical's bankruptcy, the site was known as the New York Seaplane Airport. In 1937, Pan American Airways took over the site and operated Sikorsky S-42s on flights to Bermuda and, in 1939, Boeing 314 Clippers on transatlantic flights.

TRANSATLANTIC PAN AMERICAN BOEING 314 TIED UP AT PORT WASHINGTON, 1939.
At the end of 1939, after a successful year, Pan American moved their seaplane operations to
New York Municipal (LaGuardia) Airport. At least one seaplane hangar remained in use, in
Port Washington, with several planes providing commuter service into Manhattan into the
early 1990s.

QUEENS SEAPLANE BASE, QUEENS, 1939–1947. Located in Whitestone, near the entrance to the East River, this base was used for flight instruction and sightseeing rides. The small base had one wooden hangar, a seaplane ramp, a dock, and five airplanes. Here a Piper J-3 Cub on floats is tied up to the base's dock *c.* 1940.

VANDERBILT ESTATE, CENTERPORT, 1936–1947. Gold Coast millionaire William K. Vanderbilt, with his waterfront estates on Long Island and in Florida, found amphibious aircraft were an excellent means of transportation. He used his amphibians to shuttle between his estates and for exotic vacations. On this estate, he built a large stucco seaplane hangar fronting Northport Bay. The hangar was advanced for its day, featuring hydraulic doors and an electric winch to move the planes onto the ramp. Here Vanderbilt's lavish Sikorsky S-43 taxis in Northport Bay.

Three
MILITARY AIRFIELDS

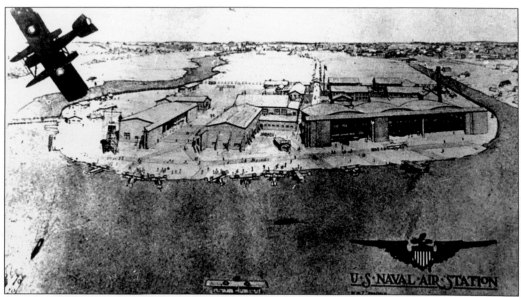

BAYSHORE NAVAL AIR STATION, BAYSHORE, 1917–1919. One of three naval air stations on Long Island during World War I, Bayshore was used for advanced training and for coastal patrol. During the 1917 federal construction program at Bayshore, 46 buildings were constructed, including housing, shops, a hospital, and five hangars. This navy artist's rendering depicts the Bayshore station in 1918. (Photograph courtesy of Long Island Maritime Museum.)

CURTISS N-9 SEAPLANE TAXIING INTO BAYSHORE, 1917. About 40 seaplanes were based here, including Curtiss R-6s, N-9s, and H and F flying boats. Approximately 800 naval aviators were trained or based here during the war. Shortly after the war, the base was closed, and many of the buildings were sold off for civilian use.

BRINDLEY FIELD, COMMACK, 1918–1919. A temporary training field and subpost of Mitchel Field, Brindley Field was hastily constructed in the spring of 1918. As there was so much flying at Mitchel and Hazelhurst Fields, this post was established to spread out the students. The 90-acre airfield featured several recycled farm buildings, as well as 20 barracks and 5 hangars. Here is the Brindley Field flight line in 1918.

BRINDLEY FIELD'S ONLY FATAL CRASH, A CURTISS JN-4, AUGUST 1918. At peak use, about 800 men were stationed on Brindley Field, and up to 40 Curtiss JN-4 training aircraft were based here. The field wound down operations and closed within months of the end of World War I.

CALVERTON AIRPORT, CALVERTON, 1954–PRESENT. In 1952, with the Grumman Corporation needing a far larger manufacturing and flight test facility, the U.S. Navy purchased 7,000 acres of land in the eastern Long Island pine barrens. This *c.* 1960 aerial view of Calverton shows the two enormous runways in a V shape, with the Grumman factory in between.

GRUMMAN F9F-6 COUGAR, THE FIRST AIRCRAFT BUILT AT CALVERTON, 1954. Originally known as the Peconic Plant, this field opened in 1954. It featured two runways, 7,000 and 10,000 feet long, two main manufacturing buildings, and eventually 100 structures as well. This Cougar sits in front of one of the main plants, with the Calverton tower behind it.

GUNNERY TEST PIT, WITH S2F TRACKER, C. 1960. Over 3,000 military aircraft were built by Grumman at what was perhaps Long Island's finest airport before the facility closed at the end of 1995.

GRUMMAN F-14A TOMCATS ON THE RAMP, CALVERTON, 1976. Calverton is still maintained, but with minimal flight operations by a skydiving school, the airport's future is uncertain.

FLOYD BENNETT FIELD, BROOKLYN, 1931–1971. New York City's first municipal airport, Floyd Bennett Field, was built on Barren Island and landfill in Jamaica Bay. This view, looking east, dates from 1936.

FORD TRIMOTOR OF UNITED AIR SERVICES, FLOYD BENNETT FIELD, 1931. One of the finest fields of its day, this field had a beautiful terminal building, four 3,000- to 4,000-foot concrete runways, eight large steel-and-concrete hangars, and a seaplane base with ramp.

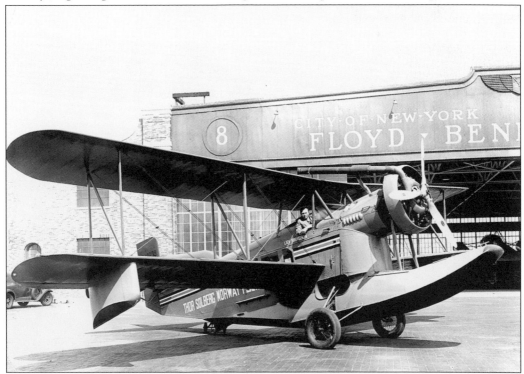

THOR SOLBERG IN HIS LOENING AMPHIBIAN, AT THE START OF HIS FLIGHT TO NORWAY, FLOYD BENNETT FIELD, 1934. Floyd Bennett Field was originally built to serve as the terminal for New York City, but this role was never realized, due to the length of time needed to traverse the distance between the field and Manhattan. Newark airport was much easier to get to.

TAYLOR CUB, FLOYD BENNETT FIELD, 1938. The opening of LaGuardia Airport in 1939 ended the little remaining commercial aviation activity on Floyd Bennett Field. (Photograph courtesy of Michael Brosnan.)

HOWARD HUGHES IN HIS LOCKHEED SUPER ELECTRA ARRIVING AT FLOYD BENNETT FIELD, 1938. Due to its fine facilities and proximity to New York City, Floyd Bennett Field provided the stage for over 40 record-breaking flights. Here Hughes has just set a new around-the-world speed record.

Vought SBUs of the Naval Reserve Squadron, Floyd Bennett Field, c. 1938. In 1941, the U.S. Navy purchased Floyd Bennett Field and immediately transformed it into a major naval air station.

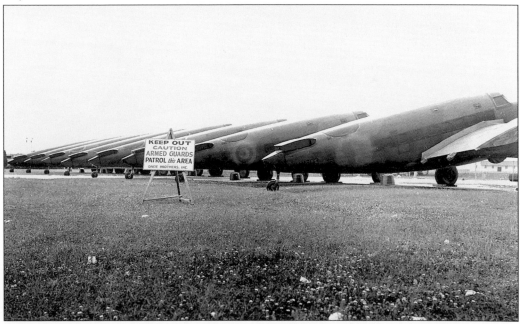

Preparing Royal Air Force Lockheed Hudsons for Shipment to England, 1942. During World War II, Floyd Bennett Field saw intensive use for antisubmarine patrols, flight training, military aircraft shipping, and ferrying operations.

LOCKHEED P2V NEPTUNE OF THE NAVAL RESERVE SQUADRON, 1958. Floyd Bennett Field remained a naval reserve base until its closing in the early 1970s.

GRUMMAN AIRPORT, BETHPAGE, 1937–1989. Having outgrown their Farmingdale facility, and with many new orders for fighters and amphibians, Grumman purchased 120 acres of land in Bethpage in 1936. This view, looking northeast, shows the factory and the grass airfield in 1938. (Photograph courtesy of the Northrop Grumman History Center.)

GRUMMAN'S FIRST FACTORY BUILDING, PLANT 1, BETHPAGE, C. 1938. The irregular rectangular airfield was formerly potato fields. By 1937, construction of the airport and factory was complete, and Grumman moved in. (Photograph courtesy of the Northrop Grumman History Center.)

NEW F6F HELLCATS PARKED ON GRUMMAN'S AIRFIELD, 1944. In the late 1930s and early 1940s, new office, factory, and hangar space was steadily added, including two 900,000-square-foot main factory buildings. The grass field also expanded to over 500 acres, including two paved runways by 1941. In March 1945, Grumman produced a record 664 aircraft in one month. (Photograph courtesy of the Northrop Grumman History Center.)

HU-16 ALBATROSS PARKED NEAR THE BETHPAGE CONTROL TOWER, C. 1960. The Grumman complex eventually contained some 75 buildings, housing 25,000 employees. The development of jets mandated changes to the flight facility; thus, by the late 1950s, only one runway was used, and it was increased to 6,500 feet. (Photograph courtesy of the Northrop Grumman History Center.)

GRUMMAN AIRPORT SURROUNDED BY A SEA OF HOUSES, 1965. As the Bethpage complex was still too small to handle new orders and jets, a much larger tract of land was secured at Calverton in the early 1950s. Grumman ceased manufacturing and flight operations at Bethpage in the late 1980s, although their administrative and engineering offices still remain there. (Photograph courtesy of the Northrop Grumman History Center.)

GYRODYNE FIELD, ST. JAMES, 1951–1970. This 320-acre landscaped estate, originally known as Flowerfield, was purchased in 1951 by the Gyrodyne Company of America for the manufacture of innovative coaxial helicopters. Here is the factory and test area of Gyrodyne, in the foreground, *c.* 1965.

GYRODYNE XRON, A SMALL ONE-MAN RECONNAISSANCE HELICOPTER OVER FLOWERFIELD, *c.* **1960.** Gyrodyne built a factory complex with an adjacent helicopter test and flying field, and they produced about 750 helicopters through 1970. Gyrodyne pioneered helicopters with two sets of counter-rotating blades, so no tail rotor was needed.

GYRODYNE QH-50 DRONE HELICOPTER WITH TORPEDOES IN THE FLIGHT TEST AREA, c. 1968. These were the world's first unmanned, armed helicopters. This property has since been redeveloped for light industry.

HAZELHURST FIELD, GARDEN CITY, 1917–1919. After taking over the Hempstead Plains Airfield in 1916, the army transformed the field into one of the largest and most important military airfields in the country. The field was renamed Hazelhurst Field in 1917, in honor of a deceased aviator. This view, looking north, dates from c. 1918. New barracks are in the foreground, with the original 1911 Hempstead Plains hangars in the distance.

HANGAR ROW AT HAZELHURST FIELD, 1918. The field became an important flight training center for army fliers, mostly using Curtiss JN-4s, as seen here. It was also given the role of an important testing station for the air service.

PUSHING OUT THE ITALIAN CAPRONI BOMBER, HAZELHURST FIELD, 1918. Almost any piece of equipment that could be put on an airplane was first tried here, including instruments, cameras, flight apparel, bombs, bombsights, stabilization devices, rockets, and radios, as well as foreign types of bombers themselves.

STUDENT AND HIS CURTISS JN-4 AT HAZELHURST FIELD, 1917. During World War I, many new buildings were constructed here, including offices, barracks, hangars, workshops, clubs, and mess halls. Over 85 aircraft were based on the field, and hundreds of military aviators were trained here during the war.

DH-4 MAIL PLANE LANDING AT HAZELHURST FIELD, 1920. After the war, the field was sold to the Curtiss Corporation, which had built a large factory on the south side of the field in 1917. The field was also the New York terminus for airmail operations between 1920 and 1925.

HUNTINGTON BAY, HUNTINGTON, 1917–1919. The U.S. Naval Aviation Reserve began on Long Island during World War I. In 1917, the Yale Unit was organized by F. Trubee Davison. This group was composed of volunteer college men who wanted to serve and fly in the navy; thus, they formed their own reserve squadron with official support. They began their naval aviation training on Curtiss flying boats in Huntington Harbor. Here a Curtiss F boat sits in the water at Huntington in 1917.

CROWDED RAMP OF THE YALE UNIT ON HUNTINGTON BAY, 1918. Seaplane facilities built here included workshops, hangars, and ramps, all constructed with private funding. By 1918, at least eight flying boats and seaplanes were based here, and the first group of volunteers was sent overseas for combat duty. The aircraft seen here are Curtiss F-type flying boats and R-type seaplanes.

MITCHEL FIELD, GARDEN CITY, 1917–1961. In 1917, a new army aviation field, known as Field No. 2, was established on the open Hempstead Plains, just south of Hazelhurst Field, to serve as an additional training base. Here we look south, across Field No. 2 and the Hempstead Plains, in 1917.

HEADQUARTERS BUILDING WITH MITCHEL FIELD OFFICERS, 1918. Numerous wooden buildings and hangars were constructed, making this 280-acre grass field one of the largest flight training airfields in the United States during World War I. In 1918, it was named Mitchel Field after former New York City mayor John P. Mitchel, who was killed during flight training in Louisiana.

LOOKING WEST ACROSS MITCHEL FIELD, 1924. All the World War I hangars and barracks seen here are still in place. Note how the hangar roofs spell out "Mitchel." Between 1929 and 1932, a major building program saw the construction of new barracks, clubs, operations buildings, workshops, 6,000-foot concrete runways, and eight massive steel and brick hangars.

CURTISS B-2 CONDOR BOMBER, MITCHEL FIELD, 1929. Mitchel Field hosted the 1920 and 1925 National Air Races and was the scene of several important long-range and endurance flights. In 1929 and 1930, it was the home of the Full Flight Laboratory, where the first instruments for blind flying were developed.

CURTISS A-8 SHRIKE ATTACK PLANE NEAR THE NEW HANGARS AT MITCHEL FIELD, 1933. Several of these hangars survive today, though in modified form.

VIEW OF MITCHEL HEADQUARTERS BUILDING AND PARADE GROUNDS, LOOKING NORTH, 1936. Off to both sides in this photograph, we see base housing, with neighboring Roosevelt Field in the upper left corner.

VIEW OF MITCHEL FIELD, LOOKING NORTH, 1940. The parked aircraft seen here are Curtiss P-40 fighters. Enlisted men's barracks are in the center, with officers' housing beyond.

B-25 Mitchell Bombers Preparing to Take Off for Antisubmarine Patrol, 1941. During World War II, Mitchel Field was the main point of air defense for New York City, a major base for antisubmarine patrols, and the main jumping-off point for bomber squadrons going to Europe.

P-82 Twin Mustang Night Fighter Squadron, Mitchel Field, 1950. Through the 1950s, Mitchel was home to an important troop carrier wing, as well as to the Continental Air Command.

AERIAL VIEW OF MITCHEL FIELD, 1955. This field is now surrounded by a sea of houses. The aircraft are Fairchild C-119s, which were used for military airlift. Due to suburban encroachment and several notable air crashes, the field was closed in 1961, and the site was redeveloped for commercial, educational, and cultural purposes.

MONTAUK NAVAL AIR STATION, MONTAUK, 1917–1919. The U.S. Navy developed an important air station at Montauk during World War I, as the site was strategically placed for monitoring shipping going in and out of New York, as well as for antisubmarine patrol. This aerial view of Montauk Naval Air Station in 1918 shows its many buildings, and the large airship hangar, amidst desolate surroundings. (Photograph courtesy of Montauk Public Library.)

PUSHING A CURTISS R-6 SEAPLANE DOWN THE RAMP AT MONTAUK NAVAL AIR STATION, 1918. Located on a 33-acre plot of land on Fort Pond, this base became operational in the summer of 1917. It possessed a 250-foot-long dirigible hangar, a seaplane hangar, shops, a hospital, a power plant, and housing for 400 men. (Photograph courtesy of Montauk Public Library.)

NAVY C-5 AIRSHIP AT MONTAUK, 1919. This airship made a record-setting nonstop flight to Nova Scotia as part of an aborted transatlantic flight. By 1918, there were 15 seaplanes stationed at Montauk, including large Curtiss HS2L flying boats and two dirigibles. With the end of the war, patrol work subsided, and by 1921, all buildings were demolished.

ROCKAWAY NAVAL AIR STATION, QUEENS, 1917–1929. Located on a narrow peninsula between the Atlantic Ocean and Jamaica Bay, this base was founded as one of three naval air stations on Long Island during World War I. This view shows the NC-10 flying boat parked on the ramp, in front of one of Rockaway's huge hangars.

VOUGHT CORSAIR ON FLOATS, ROCKAWAY, 1931. Over 80 buildings—including seaplane hangars, a 250-foot-long airship hangar, and housing for over 1,200 men—were constructed on this 96-acre site. The base housed seaplanes, floatplanes, airships, and kite balloons and was used for antisubmarine patrol and advanced training.

NAVY CURTISS NC-4 FLYING BOAT ON THE BEACH AT ROCKAWAY, 1919. This base was also the home of Seaplane Division 1, and it was from here that the NC-4 departed on its historic transatlantic flight in May 1919.

AIRSHIP AT ROCKAWAY, HAULED OUT FOR A FLIGHT, 1919. By the mid-1920s, most flying operations at Rockaway had ceased, and in 1930, the site was turned over to the city of New York. It is now known as Jacob Riis Park.

Four

GENERAL AVIATION
AIRPORTS

AVIATION COUNTRY CLUB, HICKSVILLE, 1929–1950. Probably the most unique airfield on Long Island, this was a private and exclusive country club that catered to wealthy and famous aviators and industrialists. It had two large hangars, a clubhouse with eight bedrooms, a bar, restaurant, pool, and tennis courts, not to mention the smooth grass flying field. The rectangular field, as seen here, measured 2,200 by 1,400 feet, with the club and pool on the lower left, and the hangars on the right. Hicksville was a general aviation airfield—that is, all flying other than military or commercial.

VIEW OF THE AVIATION COUNTRY CLUB, LOOKING SOUTH, 1936. The best private planes of the day could be seen on the club's field, and every year a private airshow featured demonstrations of new military, private, and business aircraft. Up to 25 planes could be stored in the hangar. The club was unable to make a go of it after World War II, and the land was sold off to become part of Levittown.

BARREN ISLAND AIRPORT, BROOKLYN, 1927–1931. Founded by Paul Rizzo on a wind-swept island in Jamaica Bay, this airport never housed more than six or eight planes. The main attraction of the field was its weekend airshows and sightseeing rides over Manhattan. This same island was later chosen as the site for Floyd Bennett Field. Here wing walkers perform on Rizzo's Waco 10 over desolate Barren Island c. 1930.

BENDER AIRPORT, 1929–1952. Founded in the late 1920s and originally known as the Central Islip Field, this airport was taken over by Henry Bender in 1933 and became known as Bender Brentwood Airport. The 33-acre grass-dirt field had one dilapidated hangar that housed three planes, with several more tied down outside. Here a Fleet Model 2 is parked in the weeds in front of the wood-tin hangar c. 1940.

BAYPORT AERODROME, BAYPORT, 1945–PRESENT. Founded in the 1940s and originally known as Davis and then Edwards Field, Bayport is the last remaining sizable general aviation grass field on Long Island. Still resembling a small 1930s airport, Bayport has one 3,200-foot-long grass-dirt runway on its 50-acre tract. Here a Fairchild PT-26 taxis past one of the original hangars at Edwards Airport in 1967.

View Looking North, Bayport, 1985. This field now houses several dozen general aviation aircraft, a flying school, and most of the planes of the Antique Airplane Club of New York. The field is now entirely surrounded by trees and houses. Here a 1937 Waco UPF-7 prepares for takeoff.

View of the Vintage 1940s Hangars at Bayport's South End, 1985. Two original metal hangars survive on this end of the field, while new T hangars are on the northeast side.

BROOKHAVEN CALABRO AIRPORT, SHIRLEY, 1944–PRESENT. Originally built in 1944 as an emergency landing strip and support facility for East Coast military aircraft, the 325-acre field was first known as Mastic Flight Strip. Brookhaven originally had a 4,200-foot-long concrete runway, with a similar second one added in 1963. Here a Curtiss Robin prepares to take off from undeveloped Mastic Flight Strip *c.* 1947.

STEARMAN CROP DUSTER AT NORTHFIELD AVIATION, BROOKHAVEN, C. 1980. The town of Brookhaven has operated this airport since 1947 and obtained ownership in 1961. (Photograph courtesy of Lynn MacDonald.)

VIEW OF BROOKHAVEN AIRPORT, LOOKING EAST, C. 1980. Construction in the 1960s and 1970s has steadily added numerous hangars, shops, fixed base operators, and a small terminal. Today about 200 general aviation aircraft and a flying school are based here. (Photograph courtesy of Bob Schmidt.)

CARLL'S SKY RANCH, COMMACK, 1929–1951. Built by John Carll, this private airfield was carved out of Carll's cattle ranch. Located on Commack Road, the field's two 2,200-foot grass strips were cut through the ranch's hayfields. Up to six planes were based on the 70-acre field and were used for personal and sightseeing use. The ranch's barn served as a hangar. The field closed upon Carll's death, and much of it has been preserved as open space. Here Carll's Travelaire is warmed up *c.* 1930.

CENTRAL PARK FLYING FIELD, BETHPAGE, 1917–1927. Also known as LWF Field and later as Junkers-Larsen Field, this airport was established during World War I on grassy plains at the southern edge of Bethpage, on Hempstead Turnpike. The Berckman's Speed Scout, seen here, was a one-of-a-kind World War I fighter prototype built at Central Park in 1917.

AIRCRAFT ENGINEERING CORPORATION ACE ON CENTRAL PARK FLYING FIELD, 1919. Surprisingly enough for a small field, at least four different aircraft manufacturing companies operated at Central Park at various times. However, not more than eight planes were housed in the field's two simple hangars at any one time. The Ace was the first post–World War I sport plane.

CORAM AIRPARK, CORAM, 1959–1985. This field consisted of two narrow, 2,000-foot dirt runways in a V layout, surrounded by tall trees on all sides. The five planes on the field were all kept outdoors, with the field's amenities consisting of one dilapidated pilot lounge-workshop. This is the view looking west down the rough dirt runway c. 1980. (Photograph courtesy of the author.)

A PIPER SUPER CUB LANDING ON CORAM'S SOUTH RUNWAY, C. 1980. Coram was operated throughout its existence by Tom Murphy, a former military flight instructor and skywriter. Tall trees at all runway ends made for interesting landings. (Photograph courtesy of the author.)

CURTISS WRIGHT FIELD, VALLEY STREAM, 1929–1947. After selling Roosevelt Field in 1929, the Curtiss Flying Service moved to a new airport they developed in Valley Stream. This new field was the second largest and busiest civil airfield on Long Island in the 1930s. Looking northwest over Curtiss Wright Airport *c.* 1930, this view shows Sunrise Highway in the upper left.

HANGAR, CURTISS WRIGHT FIELD, C. 1930. This field was to become a major aviation center, but it had the initial misfortune of opening just as the Depression struck, and it first closed in 1933. The field covered 325 acres and featured three grass runways measuring between 1,400 and 1,900 feet long. There were also seven substantial steel-and-concrete hangars.

FRANK HAWKS ARRIVING AT VALLEY STREAM IN HIS TRAVELAIRE AFTER SETTING A NEW TRANSCONTINENTAL SPEED RECORD, JULY 13, 1930. During its brief history, due to its proximity to New York City, several historic long-distance flights began or ended at Valley Stream. The field is also remembered as being the birthplace of the 99s, an international organization of women pilots.

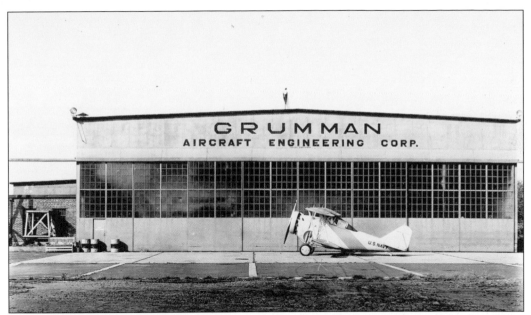

GRUMMAN FF-1 NAVY SCOUT NEAR GRUMMAN FACTORY, VALLEY STREAM, 1931. Grumman had their first real plant here in the early 1930s. The field reopened during World War II, when the Columbia Aircraft Company located their factory here and produced 330 Grumman Duck amphibians.

HANGAR AT VALLEY STREAM, WITH THE CURTISS WRIGHT LOGO, 1930. The Commonwealth Aircraft Company produced Skyrangers here through 1947, when they ceased operation. The site was sold in the 1950s and is now the Green Acres shopping mall.

DEER PARK AIRPORT, DEER PARK, 1946–1974. A medium-sized general aviation airport, Deer Park had two runways, a 2,400-foot paved one and a 1,500-foot grass strip. This aerial view was taken in 1970. (Photograph courtesy of Lou Mancuso.)

MCRAE SUPER DART AT DEER PARK, C. 1960. This field featured a flying school, three hangars, runway lighting, radio operations, and a restaurant. It befell the fate of most Long Island airports and is now a housing development. The Super Dart was an early home-built aircraft from the 1950s.

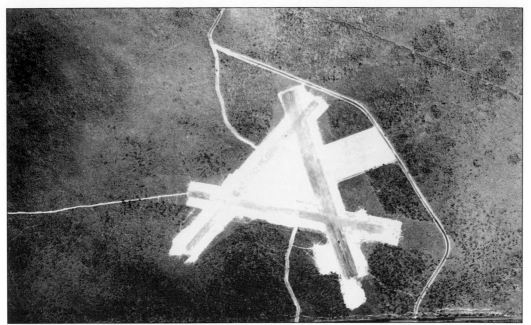

EASTHAMPTON AIRPORT, WAINSCOTT, 1937–PRESENT. Built as a Works Progress Administration project in the 1930s, this field originally had three gravel runways, each 2,500 feet long. It now features three paved runways measuring up to 4,000 feet long. After being used as an emergency strip during World War II, the field was operated by Charlotte Niles and Margaret Lowell-Wallace, two former Women's Airforce Service Pilots, through the 1950s. With four aircraft and a barracks as a terminal, the two women built up a creditable flying school and sightseeing operation. This view was taken in the late 1930s.

EASTHAMPTON AIRPORT TERMINAL, C. 1980. This terminal, once a barracks in World War II, has since been replaced by a beautiful New England–style building. The airport has 40,000 charter, corporate, and personal aircraft movements per year, mostly during the active Hamptons summer months. (Photograph courtesy of Leo Polaski.)

EAST MORICHES AIRPORT, EAST MORICHES, 1975–PRESENT. Also known as Lufker Field, this small grass strip is just west of Spadaro's Airport. Founded by Lou Lufker, it features a 2,300-foot grass runway, a metal hangar, and about 10 aircraft. It is mainly used for banner towing, ultralights, soaring, and student activity. (Photograph courtesy of Bob Schmidt.)

FITZMAURICE FIELD, MASSAPEQUA, 1929–1953. Unique in the history of Long Island's airfields, Fitzmaurice was originally envisioned as a neighborhood airfield for the rapidly growing community of Massapequa Park. In the late 1920s, developers saw it as a place where local residents could keep their planes, or use it for business purposes. This view, looking northeast, was taken in 1935. The streets for Massapequa Park have already been laid out.

FITZMAURICE FIELD HANGAR, C. 1950. This plane is a 1918 Thomas Morse Scout owned by Paul Kotze and kept on the field for many years. Basically a large open field with two short, 1,700-foot grass runways and two hangars, Fitzmaurice never achieved the potential envisioned for it, and there were never more than 25 planes on the field. Due to limited use, it was sold off for the development of two schools in 1953.

FLUSHING AIRPORT, QUEENS, 1927–1981. Founded by Anthony "Speed" Hanzlik, Flushing was the last general aviation airport within the limits of New York City. The 305-acre field, located in marshland, featured six wooden hangars, an operations building with control tower, and two paved runways, each 3,000 feet long. This view, looking northeast, was taken in 1950.

REPUBLIC SEABEE TAXIING UP TO THE FLIGHT LINE AT FLUSHING, C. 1950. By the late 1970s, Flushing handled 45,000 flights per year, including many charter and corporate operations. Its close proximity to LaGuardia Airport, two miles away, and concerns over air and residential safety, ultimately led to its closing. Most of the field is now flooded and undeveloped.

FREEPORT AIRPORT, FREEPORT, 1929–1935. This airport was intended to be an important airfield for Long Island's south shore and to help in the development of the town of Freeport. The 70-acre flying field, located on South Grove Street, consisted of two grass-dirt runways, 1,500 and 2,000 feet long, and one barnlike hangar. Although there were great plans for the field, the Depression led to its closure, and the land was sold off for housing. Here an Alexander Eaglerock visits Freeport in 1930.

FROG'S FLYING FIELD, EAST MORICHES, 1925–1941. Founded by Walter "Frog" Chapman, this small grass field never had more than five planes on it. Its one hangar had no doors, and the short runway had to be approached at a steep angle in order to clear bordering electric lines and not overshoot the field. Today it is the site of the East Moriches School. This view of the runway, looking south, was taken in 1930.

GABRESKI AIRPORT, WESTHAMPTON BEACH, 1931–PRESENT. Originally known as Suffolk Airport, this airfield was a spartan general aviation airfield through the 1930s, consisting of 350 acres, with one hangar and a 2,800- by 5,100-foot dirt flying field. This view of Suffolk Airport in the pine barrens was taken in 1938.

HANGAR, SUFFOLK AIRPORT, 1935. This airport continued to be a rather sleepy general aviation field until it was purchased by the federal government. It reopened in 1943 as the Suffolk Gunnery Training Center.

DUMMY CONVOY FOR STRAFING PRACTICE, SUFFOLK GUNNERY TRAINING CENTER, 1944.
A subpost of Mitchel Field, this center was used to train P-47 pilots in gunnery, bombing, and rocketry. The field was greatly expanded to 9,000 acres, with a 5,500-foot paved runway and numerous gunnery and bombing ranges with simulated targets.

F-102 AT SUFFOLK AIR FORCE BASE, 1968. The Suffolk Gunnery Training Center closed in 1946 but was reopened in 1951 as Suffolk Air Force Base. A new construction program gave the field three paved runways and many new hangars and support buildings. Between 1951 and 1969, several different squadrons were stationed here, providing the air defense for New York City.

AN AERIAL VIEW OF SUFFOLK COUNTY AIRPORT, LOOKING NORTHWEST, C. 1980. Suffolk Air Force Base closed in 1969, and the field was deeded to Suffolk County in 1972. Reopened as a general aviation field and known as Suffolk County Airport, it had three paved runways measuring between 5,500 and 9,000 feet long and many useable former military structures. A U.S. Air Force air-sea rescue unit remains on the field. In 1994, the airport was renamed after World War II ace Francis Gabreski.

GULF FIELD, HICKSVILLE, 1935–1948. This was basically a large open field with no structures and was little more than a place to hold the overflow student traffic from Roosevelt Field. It was known as Gulf Field after the gas truck that was often parked there. Instructors took their students here because the gas was cheaper than at Roosevelt Field and there was less air traffic. Today the site is part of Levittown.

HAMPTON AIRPORT, BRIDGEHAMPTON, 1929–1946. Located between Bridgehampton and Southampton, this field was also known as Haygrounds Airport. It was a small, 75-acre grass strip, in an unusual T layout. This view, looking southwest, was taken in 1935.

BOOTLEGGING OPERATIONS AT HAMPTON AIRPORT, C. 1930. This field featured two grass runways, each about 1,600 feet long, and one hangar. Like many Long Island airports, it participated in the bootlegging trade during Prohibition. The hangar still remains and is used for agricultural purposes.

HICKSVILLE AIR PARK, SYOSSET, 1945–1949. Founded by George Spohrer, this 35-acre field, located on Robbins Lane, lasted fewer than five years. Throughout the field's existence, contentious legal battles raged between Spohrer and the town board. The field featured one hangar, an office, and about 15 aircraft. Flying lessons were given by veterans. The entire site was eventually turned into an industrial park. Here an unusual Ryan SCW-145 is parked on the field in 1947.

HOLMES AIRPORT, QUEENS, 1928–1940. This civil field was unique in that it had facilities for both airplanes and airships. Located in Jackson Heights only three miles east of Times Square, it was intended to be the major general aviation field for New York. It had two hangars and an office. It was 220 acres of dirt, with two gravel runways of 2,800 and 3,000 feet in length. This view of the field, taken after the removal of the airship hangar, looks southwest toward neighboring LaGuardia Airport in 1939.

PIPER J-3 CUB AT HOLMES AIRPORT, 1938. This field was also the base for the first scheduled airline that operated from New York City, with an Eastern Air Express Ford Trimotor making the two-day run to Miami, beginning in 1929.

AIRSHIP ENTERPRISE LANDING AT HOLMES AIRPORT, 1933. The 220-foot-long airship hangar was completed in 1931 and housed Goodyear airships through 1935. The airships were used for aerial advertising and the first airborne traffic reports. Due to financial problems and the opening of nearby New York Municipal (LaGuardia) Airport in 1939, the field was closed and the land sold for a housing project.

ISLIP AIRPORT, ISLIP, 1928–1947. Surprisingly, this small, 25-acre field was Long Island's first municipal airport. It had two 2,000-foot-long grass runways on a rectangular field, with one steel hangar. The field was founded by Charles Lawrance, designer of the Wright radial engines, and it opened to great fanfare, including a dedication by Amelia Earhart. In this 1938 photograph, we see Route 111 running along the top.

SUFFOLK COUNTY'S FIRST AIRMAIL FLIGHT, ISLIP AIRPORT, MAY 19, 1938. Here we see Mayor Walker of Brightwaters posing with pilot William Thies and his Travelaire 6000B. Other than a flying school, there was little action on this field, and hoped-for growth never materialized. It was sold for use as an automobile racetrack following World War II. The site is now an industrial park. (Photograph courtesy of Dick Milligan.)

JAMAICA SEA AIRPORT, QUEENS, 1927–1942. Located on a tiny sand spit in Jamaica Bay, this was the first airport to open on city land in Queens. Founded by Martin Devereaux, the field's primary function was operating sightseeing flights over Queens and Brooklyn. Here a Savoia-Marchetti S-56 rests at the airport in 1935. Cross Bay Boulevard is in the distance.

CURTISS JENNY AT JAMAICA SEA AIRPORT, C. 1927. This scruffy field, housing about eight planes, had three dirt runways measuring between 1,500 and 3,000 feet long, one tin hangar, an office, and a seaplane ramp on the bay. The site was later taken back by New York City and leveled for the construction of New York International (Kennedy) Airport in 1942.

MacArthur Airport, Islip, 1942–Present. First established as a defense landing area by the federal government, this airport served the many military aircraft being built on Long Island. The field opened in 1943, with three 5,000-foot concrete runways, and was named after Gen. Douglas MacArthur in 1945. This aerial view shows the defense landing area in 1944.

Original Terminal, MacArthur Airport, 1951. After World War II, the town of Islip took over the airport, and by the early 1960s, airline service began. The airport expanded, and a new terminal and control tower were built. Here, parked in front of the original terminal, we see a Lockheed Hudson, BT-13, Grumman Goose, and a Beech 18.

MacArthur Airport Flight Line, c. 1965. Here we can see the Sperry facility in the foreground, with the original terminal in the distance. By the 1990s, with the addition of Southwest Airlines, MacArthur had become an important feeder center.

Sperry Facility, MacArthur Airport, c. 1950. Between 1945 and 1965, the Sperry Gyroscope Corporation based their flight operations at MacArthur, developing remote-controlled aircraft, as well as many new radars, instruments, and instrument landing systems. Here we see DC-3s, a B-17, and a B-29 parked in front of the Sperry hangar.

SF-340 COMMUTER AT THE NEW MACARTHUR TERMINAL, C. 1990. This 1,311-acre airport is also home to many corporate jet aircraft and has expanded to the point that it is the third busiest airport in New York State. The airport became known as Long Island MacArthur Airport in 1978 to reflect its regional service area.

MATTITUCK AIRBASE, MATTITUCK, 1945–PRESENT. This airstrip remains relatively unchanged since it was founded by Parker Wickham in the mid-1940s. It has two hangars, a 2,200-foot paved runway, and a seaplane ramp bordering Peconic Bay. Here we see a Cessna 170 amphibian parked at Mattituck c. 1970.

VIEW OF THE HANGARS AND WORKSHOPS AT MATTITUCK, C. 1952. Although it houses several dozen aircraft, Mattituck is primarily known as an important center for aircraft engine overhaul and modification. An interesting assortment of aircraft can be seen parked here in the field's early days, including a privately owned P-38 and two DC-3s. (Photograph courtesy of Parker Wickham.)

NASSAU AIRPORT, EAST MEADOW, 1938–1947. This 100-acre grass field was located on Hempstead Turnpike. Its single wooden hangar was originally the World War I mess hall for the army's nearby Camp Mills. In addition to the lone structure, the field had three grass runways measuring between 1,900 and 2,800 feet long. Here a Porterfield sits on the field *c.* 1946.

PORTERFIELD, NOSED OVER ON RUTTY NASSAU AIRPORT, 1946. This field was used for flight instruction and for giving sightseeing rides. It was eventually sold for development, as neighboring Levittown was booming after World War II.

NORTH BEACH AIRPORT, QUEENS, 1928–1937. This field was originally developed in the late 1920s as a seaplane base by New York Air Terminals. In the 1930s, it was bought and further developed by the Curtiss Wright Company. It was known for a period as Glenn Curtiss Airport. This aerial view of North Beach, looking north, was taken in 1932. (Photograph courtesy of the Port Authority of New York and New Jersey.)

NEW YORK POLICE AVIATION UNIT AT NORTH BEACH, 1930. This field saw seasonal airline operations to resort areas in the early 1930s and was the base for the New York Police Department Aviation Unit. Seen here are Keystone Loening and Savoia Marchetti amphibians.

GERMAN DORNIER DO-X FLYING BOAT TAXIING INTO NORTH BEACH AFTER CROSSING THE ATLANTIC, 1932. This field consisted of 230 acres with three steel hangars, an operations building, and three oiled gravel runways between 2,200 and 2,500 feet in length. Advanced for its day, the field was fully lighted for night flying and had radio communication and a weather station.

FORD TRIMOTOR, USED ON ATLANTIC CITY RUNS, NORTH BEACH, 1930. At its peak, this field housed 70 aircraft, flying schools, and aircraft sales businesses. The field was sold in 1937 for the development of New York Municipal (LaGuardia) Airport.

REPUBLIC AIRPORT, FARMINGDALE, 1928–PRESENT. Opened in the late 1920s, this was originally known as Fairchild Flying Field. The Fairchild Company of Farmingdale built large photographic and transport monoplanes, and they purchased this 100-acre site for their factory and airport. Here we see the grass field that later became Republic Airport, looking northeast, 1935.

FAIRCHILD COMPANY HANGAR WITH FAIRCHILD PRODUCTS, FARMINGDALE, C. 1930.
Fairchild Flying Field originally contained the nine-building Fairchild plant and two 4,000-foot
grass runways.

GRUMMAN FF-1 ON AMERICAN (REPUBLIC) AIRPORT, 1933. After Fairchild moved to
Maryland in 1932, the field was known as American Airport. Grumman built fighter and
amphibious aircraft here between 1931 and 1937.

FORMER FAIRCHILD FACTORY, NOW OCCUPIED BY SEVERSKY, 1937. The Seversky Aircraft Corporation set up its factory here in 1935, and American Airport then became known as Seversky Airport.

NEW SEVERSKY P-35 FIGHTERS ON THE FIELD, FARMINGDALE, 1937. Seversky built fighters, trainers, and amphibious planes here through 1939, when the company's—and the airport's— name was changed to Republic.

NEW REPUBLIC P-47 THUNDERBOLT FIGHTERS PARKED ON THE FARMINGDALE FIELD, 1944.
Republic's 25,000 employees built over 10,000 P-47s here during World War II.

BRITISH EXPORT P-47 TAKES OFF, FARMINGDALE, 1945. The flight test hangar and control tower are seen in the rear of this photograph. The P-47 fighter-bomber was one of the best aircraft produced during World War II.

REPUBLIC F-105 THUNDERCHIEF ROLLOUT, FARMINGDALE, 1957. Into the 1980s, Republic produced many notable aircraft here, including the F-84, F-105, and A-10. The airport has kept the name Republic, even though the corporation closed its doors in 1987. The field changed from private to public in 1966. It now encompasses some 500 acres and is home to 500 aircraft. It is the busiest general aviation airport in New York State.

VIEW OF REPUBLIC AIRPORT, LOOKING NORTH, C. 1965. This field handles private planes, corporate jets, and midsized airliners. The complex includes an instrument landing system, two concrete runways of 6,600 and 7,500 feet in length, and many aviation businesses. This is Long Island's oldest surviving airport. The field is basically unchanged today, except that the factory complex seen at the top of this photograph has been replaced by a shopping center.

RIVERHEAD AIRPARK, RIVERHEAD, 1946–1963. Located on Sound Avenue, this small airport consisted of one 2,000-foot grass strip. It also had two tin Quonset hut hangars and an office. Originally started to service crop dusters, it eventually came to house about 15 aircraft. Here a Grumman Agcat crop duster lands at Riverhead *c.* 1960.

ROCKAWAY AIRPORT, ROCKAWAY, 1940–1958. Located in a marshy area in Edgemere, on the northeast side of Jamaica Bay, this served as a small general aviation airport. It had two 2,200-foot cinder runways surrounded by marsh grass, and one tin hangar. Here a Waco biplane visits Rockaway *c.* 1947.

ROOSEVELT FIELD, GARDEN CITY, 1919–1951. This was by far the largest and most colorful Long Island airfield during aviation's golden age. Formerly Hazelhurst Field, it was renamed after Theodore Roosevelt's deceased son, Quentin, in 1919. In 1920, the 700-acre field was divided in half, with the western half being sold to the Curtiss Company and renamed Curtiss Field. In this photograph of a 1921 flying festival at Curtiss Field, all the remaining buildings date from World War I or earlier.

ENTRANCE TO CURTISS FIELD, GARDEN CITY, 1926. Most of this field was occupied by the Curtiss Flying Service, which included aircraft sales, service, a flying school, and flight testing of Curtiss products. Visible in the rear is the Sikorsky S-29 that later crashed and burned while making a transatlantic flight attempt.

CHARLES LINDBERGH'S *SPIRIT OF ST. LOUIS*, TAKEN OUT FOR A TEST FLIGHT, CURTISS FIELD, MAY 1927. The historic transatlantic flights of the late 1920s, including Lindbergh's, took place from the less developed eastern field, as it had a much longer runway.

ROOSEVELT FIELD AT ITS PEAK, C. 1935. In 1929, Roosevelt Field Inc. bought Curtiss Field back and recombined the two fields into one, known again as Roosevelt Field. In 1935, the eastern half was again sold, this time to become an automobile racetrack. The row of concrete hangars lines the north side of the field.

VIEW OF THE ACTIVE FLIGHT LINE AT ROOSEVELT FIELD. A major construction program in 1929–1930 gave the western field paved runways, many concrete hangars, a hotel, restaurant, radio station, and night flying lighting. This field was the scene of numerous historic flights through the 1930s, including those for altitude, endurance, transcontinental, transatlantic, and around-the-world speed records. This photograph dates from 1935.

CURTISS ROBIN TAKING OFF OVER THE 1911 HANGARS REMAINING FROM HEMPSTEAD PLAINS AIRFIELD, ROOSEVELT FIELD, C. 1930. The 500-acre field housed over 450 planes with 150 aviation businesses and boasted 3 asphalt runways of 2,000 feet each. At the time, this was America's largest and busiest civil airfield.

GRUMMAN F4Fs BEING MODIFIED FOR BRITISH SERVICE, ROOSEVELT FIELD, 1943. During World War II, the U.S. Navy took over the field and operated a mechanics' school there. The British Royal Navy also set up a station to modify American aircraft for use on British aircraft carriers.

THE END OF THE LINE, NOW QUIET ROOSEVELT FIELD, LOOKING WEST, 1950. After World War II, civil aviation tapered off drastically, and this field could no longer support itself. In 1951, the site was sold for development as a shopping mall.

ROSE FIELD, ORIENT, 1937–1999. Founded by Charles Rose in the late 1930s, this 1,500-foot grass strip never housed more than three aircraft. It had one metal hangar, and the north end of the runway ended at Long Island Sound. This view, looking north, was taken in 1985. (Photograph courtesy of Bob Schmidt.)

SAYVILLE AIRPORT, SAYVILLE, 1928–1952. Founded by Karl Pausewang, this tiny grass field never housed more than six aircraft. It consisted of a 1,500- by 700-foot rectangle with one wooden hangar. The 22-acre field was entirely surrounded by trees. Today the field is the site of the Lincoln Avenue School. Here Pausewang's Curtiss Jenny prepares for takeoff c. 1930.

SHELTER ISLAND AIRPORT, SHELTER ISLAND, 1962–PRESENT. Built by Frank Klenawickus, this small airstrip has a 1,700-foot grass runway, one hangar, and four aircraft. Here a Piper Tri-Pacer approaches for landing *c.* 1965.

SKY PORTAL, MONTAUK, 1958–PRESENT. Owned by Suffolk County, this small airport is basically a seasonal operation and is used from spring through fall by vacationing pilots and by tourists on their way to the east end of Long Island. It has an office, one metal hangar, and a 3,500-foot lighted asphalt runway. This aerial view, looking southwest, dates from 2001. (Photograph courtesy of Montauk Public Library.)

SPADARO'S AIRPORT, EAST MORICHES, 1960–PRESENT. Founded by Bart Spadaro on a chicken farm, this airport now has a 2,200-foot asphalt runway, paved taxiway, and eight metal hangars. It is home to about 30 aircraft. The major activities here are sightseeing rides, soaring, skydiving, and flight training. In this view, looking south, Spadaro's is on the left, and the grass strip of East Moriches Airport is to its immediate right. No two airports on Long Island have ever been closer together than these. (Photograph courtesy of Bart Spadaro.)

SMITHTOWN AVIATION COUNTRY CLUB, SMITHTOWN, 1952–1957. Built on the grounds of an old farm, this field had one grass runway and six T hangars. Members and their guests could stay overnight in the old farmhouse, which also had a pool. At most, about 20 planes were based here. Always in financial difficulty, the field, located on Nesconset Highway, was eventually sold to Suffolk County, and the site was developed into courthouses. Here we see a Stinson Voyager resting on the country club field in 1955. (Photograph courtesy of Hank Anholzer.)

TALMAGE AIRSTRIP, RIVERHEAD, 1967–PRESENT. John Talmage built this private airstrip, the last one on Long Island, on his potato farm. The strip is 2,000 feet of well-manicured sod, with one metal hangar. The field hosts an annual "fly in" of antique aircraft, as seen here.

ZAHN'S AIRPORT, AMITYVILLE, 1936–1980. This airport began in the mid-1930s as a 1,000-foot dirt strip plowed through an orchard on Joseph Zahn's farm. This aerial view was taken in 1965.

PIPER CUB ON SKIS AT ZAHN'S, C. 1960. Zahn was bought out by Ed Lyons, Jack Looney, and Walter Hoffman in 1950, and the field was steadily improved through the 1950s. With the closure of Roosevelt Field in 1951, Zahn's became the busiest general aviation airport in New York State.

SKYVIEWS B-17 BASED AT ZAHN'S, 1955. At its peak, almost 300 aircraft were based here, with 300,000 aircraft movements annually. The 130-acre airport had many hangars, workshops, offices, a radio, and two paved, lighted runways of 3,000 and 5,000 feet in length. This B-17 was used for aerial photography in the 1950s. (Photograph courtesy of John Golden.)

ZAHN'S AIRPORT'S LARGEST HANGAR, 1975. Despite the fact that it also housed a New York Air National Guard unit, by the late 1960s, Zahn's revenue declined steadily, and the field began to deteriorate. Rising taxes made the field uneconomical, and the site was purchased in 1980 by the town of Babylon for an industrial park.

Five

COMMERCIAL AIRPORTS

JOHN F. KENNEDY INTERNATIONAL, QUEENS, 1948–PRESENT. Not long after the completion of New York Municipal (LaGuardia) Airport, city officials realized that they needed yet another new airport to handle more cargo, larger and faster airplanes, and many more of them. This view of brand-new New York International, looking south, was taken in 1948. (Photograph courtesy of the Port Authority of New York and New Jersey.)

INSIDE THE CONTROL TOWER, NEW YORK INTERNATIONAL, OPENING DAY, JUNE 1, 1948. This airport was built on marshland and landfill in Jamaica Bay. The original airport consisted of a temporary terminal building and Quonset huts, but there was tremendous room for expansion. (Photograph courtesy of the Port Authority of New York and New Jersey.)

ORIGINAL TERMINAL AND CONTROL TOWER, NEW YORK INTERNATIONAL, 1952. When it opened, this was the East Coast's only major aerial gateway into the United States. During the 1950s, the airport, also known as Idlewild, became the first really large-scale airport in the world. In this photograph, the airport's second control tower is under construction in the distance. Note the rooftop promenade. (Photograph courtesy of the Port Authority of New York and New Jersey.)

ORIGINAL TERMINAL WITH QUONSET HUT GATE AREA, NEW YORK INTERNATIONAL, 1953.
In the 1950s, with six operations per minute, this was the world's busiest airport. The aircraft seen here are Lockheed Constellations, Boeing B-377s, and DC-6s. Passengers walked across the tarmac to get to their planes. (Photograph courtesy of the Port Authority of New York and New Jersey.)

ELEVATED TAXIWAY, NEW YORK INTERNATIONAL, 1948. An unusual feature of this airport, which exists to this day, is that cars drive under the taxiway when entering the airport. The aircraft seen here is an Air France Lockheed Constellation. (Photograph courtesy of the Port Authority of New York and New Jersey.)

INTERNATIONAL ARRIVALS BUILDING, EAST AND WEST WINGS, AND SECOND CONTROL TOWER, NEW YORK INTERNATIONAL, 1958. This arrivals building, opened in 1957, was replaced by a larger, more modern complex in 2002. The original terminal and control tower are in the foreground of this view. (Photograph courtesy of the Port Authority of New York and New Jersey.)

PAN AMERICAN BOEING 707, THE FIRST COMMERCIAL JET FLIGHT, NEW YORK INTERNATIONAL, SEPTEMBER 1958. By the late 1960s, the airport grew to over 5,000 acres—as large as Manhattan from its tip to 42nd Street. (Photograph courtesy of the Port Authority of New York and New Jersey.)

JOHN F. KENNEDY INTERNATIONAL AIRPORT'S THIRD, AND THE WORLD'S TALLEST, CONTROL TOWER, 1995. Rededicated as Kennedy International Airport in 1963, this airport now handles almost 30 million passengers per year, as well as 1.5 million tons of cargo. (Photograph courtesy of the Port Authority of New York and New Jersey.)

AERIAL VIEW OF JOHN F. KENNEDY INTERNATIONAL, 1995. In addition to the international arrivals building, the airport also has 10 separate passenger terminals. The runway system consists of two pairs of parallel runways, set at right angles, each measuring 10,000 to 14,000 feet long (among the world's longest), with 22 miles of taxiways. (Photograph courtesy of the Port Authority of New York and New Jersey.)

LaGuardia Airport, Queens, 1939–Present. Here we see the opening-day ceremonies at LaGuardia on October 15, 1939. Due to the commercial failure of Floyd Bennett Field, in the late 1930s, construction began on a new airport, New York Municipal, on the site of the old Glenn Curtiss Airport at North Beach. Landfill created this 558-acre airport on Flushing Bay, on a main highway, with unobstructed water approaches. The boat basin in the upper right, now long gone, was for ferry service to Manhattan. (Photograph courtesy of the Port Authority of New York and New Jersey.)

THE LANDPLANE ADMINISTRATION BUILDING, NEW YORK MUNICIPAL AIRPORT. Completed under a $40 million Works Progress Administration project, the new airport opened for the New York World's Fair in 1939. In the 1940s, the airport came to be known as LaGuardia, after the popular mayor who promoted its construction. The airport had seven huge hangars, a passenger terminal, seaplane base, and four runways, one of which was 6,000 feet long, the longest in the world at that time. This building was demolished in 1962. (Photograph courtesy of the Port Authority of New York and New Jersey.)

THE MARINE AIR TERMINAL AND SEAPLANE HANGAR ON FLUSHING BAY, NEW YORK MUNICIPAL, 1940. By 1940, all commercial Pan American flying boat activity moved from Port Washington to the new Marine Air Terminal at LaGuardia. (Photograph courtesy of the Port Authority of New York and New Jersey.)

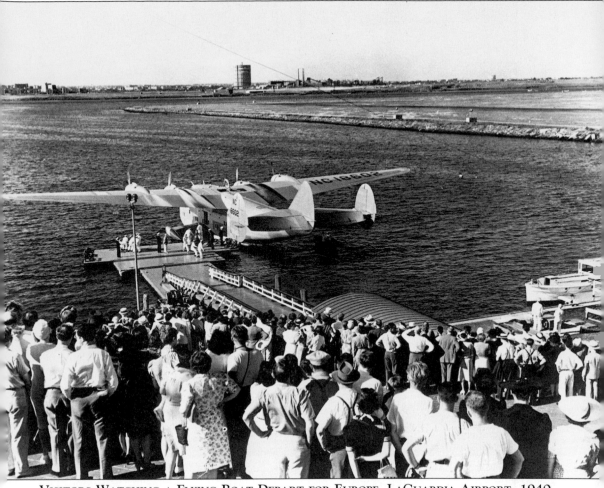

Visitors Watching a Flying Boat Depart for Europe, LaGuardia Airport, 1940.
The occasion shown in this photograph is the departure of the first Pan American transatlantic flying boat, a Boeing 314, on March 30, 1940.

AERIAL VIEW OF LAGUARDIA AIRPORT, LOOKING NORTHWEST, C. 1946. During the 1940s, LaGuardia was the busiest airport in the country. It handled 197,000 flights in 1946 alone. This view was taken before the runways were extended into the bay and the boat basin filled in for parking. The hangars were the largest in the world at the time. (Photograph courtesy of the Port Authority of New York and New Jersey.)

"Skywalk" Observation Deck at LaGuardia Airport, c. 1948. On nice weekends, as many as 25,000 people visited the airport just to watch planes take off and land. (Photograph courtesy of the Port Authority of New York and New Jersey.)

LaGuardia Airport, Looking Southeast, c. 1951. In the 1950s, LaGuardia was redeveloped with a new passenger terminal, control tower, parking areas, and roadway system. The original control tower is visible on top of the administration building in the center. The first boarding gates extending onto the ramp can also be seen. The aircraft are Convair 220s and DC-6s. (Photograph courtesy of the Port Authority of New York and New Jersey.)

SECOND CONTROL TOWER (1962) AND BOEING 737S AT LAGUARDIA AIRPORT, 1984.
In the 1960s, LaGuardia's two main runways were extended into Riker's Island Channel.
(Photograph courtesy of the Port Authority of New York and New Jersey.)

LaGuardia, Runway Extensions into Flushing Bay, c. 1985. In the 1990s, two additional passenger terminals were built. (Photograph courtesy of the Port Authority of New York and New Jersey.)